Top Tips for Toddler Tantrums

Top Tips for Toddler Tantrums

Gina Ford

Vermilion
LONDON

Published in 2011 by Vermilion, an imprint of Ebury Publishing
Ebury Publishing is a Random House Group company

[Addresse] [The Random House Group Limited Reg. No. 954009] [w]ww.randomhouse.co.uk

[A CIP catalogue record for this book is available from the Briti]sh Library

Printed and bound in Great Britain by Clays Ltd, St Ives plc

ISBN 9780091935146

To buy books by your favourite authors and register for offers, visit www.randomhouse.co.uk

The information in this book has been compiled by way of general guidance in relation to the
specific subjects addressed, but is not a substitute and not to be relied on for medical, healthcare,
pharmaceutical or other professional advice on specific circumstances and in specific locations.
Please consult your GP before changing, stopping or starting any medical treatment. So far as the
author is aware the information given is correct and up to date as at February 2011. Practice, laws
and regulations all change, and the reader should obtain up-to-date professional advice on any such
issues. The author and publishers disclaim, as far as the law allows, any liability arising directly or
indirectly from the use, or misuse, of the information contained in this book.

Contents

Acknowledgements   9

Introduction   11

1 Why Tantrums Happen   13

Key skills learned between 12 and 36 months   15

Having a second baby – age gap   21

2 Dealing with Tantrums   25

Dealing with tantrums in the second year   30

Dealing with tantrums in the third year   33

Finding the right method 51

The importance of positive praise 53

Head-banging and breath-holding 57

3 **Learning New Skills** 59

Walking 64

Talking 67

Dressing 71

4 **Food Fights** 75

A toddler's appetite 80

Ending the battle 85

5 **Bedtime Battles** 91

The importance of a routine 92

6 The Social Toddler 105

Aggressive behaviour 108

Dealing with tantrums in public 121

Conclusion 127

Useful Resources 129

Further Reading 132

Acknowledgements

I would like to express my gratitude to the thousands of parents who I have worked with or advised over the years. Their constant feedback, opinions and suggestions have been an enormous help in writing my books.

I would also like to thank my publisher Fiona MacIntyre and editor Louise Coe for their constant encouragement and faith in my work, and thanks to the rest of the team at Vermilion for all their hard work on the book.

Special thanks are also owed to my agent Emma Kirby, for her dedication and support, and to Laura Simmons, for her efforts in gathering information for the book. Thank you to Kate Brian, the website editor of Contentedbaby.com, Sophie Huthwaite, Jane Waygood and Rory Jenkins, and the rest of the team at Contentedbaby.com, for their support while I was writing this book and their wonderful work on the website.

And, finally, I am ever grateful for the huge support I receive from the thousands of readers of my books who take the time to contact me – a huge thank you to you all and much love to your contented babies.

Introduction

The toddler years can be a tremendous time for parents, yet I believe it is how parents approach this period that will govern how much they enjoy it. Children are learning so much during this stage, and their individual personalities are becoming more apparent. Each day presents so many opportunities to encourage their enthusiasm and interest in the world around them. Even the most mundane activity can provide a new adventure or challenge.

It saddens me that this very engaging period in a child's life can sometimes be portrayed as a battle of wills between the parent and the child. We hear so much about 'the terrible twos', and this can colour a parent's judgement of how to deal with a toddler's behaviour. A parent can begin this phase with the expectation that the child will manifest difficult behaviour when in fact there is nothing terrible about these years. They are the time that children experience their first steps towards independence, and the world is an exciting, but also sometimes frightening, place for them. I have rarely looked after a pre-schooler who at some stage didn't respond to a situation with a tantrum, but tantrums are simply a normal part of a child's development, which can often be avoided and can certainly be reduced with the right approach.

1
Why Tantrums Happen

We've all witnessed how distressing it can be for both the parent and a child when a toddler throws a tantrum, particularly if this happens in a public place. Pity the poor mother whose child is lying in the aisle of a supermarket screaming, or the father attempting to persuade his shrieking child to leave the playground. Both parent and child can be left looking emotionally drained and simply out of control after such an episode. Yet, the secret to raising well-behaved children is really quite simple: **establish boundaries early on and then stick to them!**

In my first book, *The New Contented Little Baby Book*, I stressed the importance of structuring a baby's feeding and sleeping habits, since many of the problems experienced by parents of young babies are food- or sleep-related, and often both. I am convinced that this is equally true of the difficulties presented by toddlers and young children. I do believe that an overtired and poorly nourished child is far more likely to suffer from behavioural and sleep-related problems, such as tantrums, nightmares and jealousy, than a child who is well rested and well fed.

During those demanding toddler years it is important that your child continues to follow a regular feeding and sleeping pattern. When this routine is combined with love, encouragement and support, your child will be in the best position to embrace the many challenges he will encounter during his first three years – and you will be in the best position to delight in his successful transition from contented baby to confident child.

Key skills learned between 12 and 36 months

A child learns more between the ages of one and three years than at any other time in his life. The learning process often ends up in tears of frustration through not being understood and sheer exhaustion from having to learn so many different things at the same time. This time often sees the arrival of a new baby, which adds fear of abandonment and feelings of jealousy to the very long list of emotions with which the toddler already has to cope.

Listed below are just a few of the main skills and challenges a toddler has to deal with in his second year:

* Learning to become more physically independent – walking and climbing.

* Learning to make his needs understood – talking.

* Learning how to make choices about what to eat and how to feed himself.

* Learning how to undress and eventually to dress himself.

* Learning how to integrate with other toddlers – playing and sharing.

By the time a toddler reaches his second birthday his walking will be much steadier and he will become more daring physically as he attempts to run, climb and jump. He will also become less frustrated mentally, because being able to string words together helps him to communicate his needs better. During the third year, however, he will be faced with a whole host of new challenges, including:

* Forming friendships with other children.

* Starting nursery school and taking instruction in a group situation.

* Learning good manners and respect for others.

* Taking more responsibility for his own actions and learning about bladder and bowel control through potty training.

During this stage of development it is important that your child learns how to think for himself and make simple decisions, so you should not do all his thinking and decision-making for him. With so many new skills to master, he is likely to get very frustrated. It is essential that social activities and sleep are carefully structured so that he doesn't become overtired; in my experience, exhausted toddlers are much more prone to having full-blown temper tantrums than those whose activities and sleep are carefully structured. Prevention is better than cure, and understanding the causes of a toddler's tantrums will go a long way in helping to avoid them.

Tantrums are a normal part of your child's development; they are his way of communicating that he can't manage. If you respond in a stressful and distressed way to your toddler's tantrum, it can compound the situation.

Creating a safe, happy and relaxed environment will help

increase your toddler's confidence during this critical stage of mental, physical and emotional development. There will be times, however, when he becomes so challenged that he finds it difficult to cope. Therefore it is essential to set very clear limits and boundaries for dealing with any difficult behaviour caused by a toddler's frustration.

The main causes of frustration that can lead to temper tantrums are:

* Difficulty communicating needs – a toddler has the mental capacity to understand virtually everything that is said to him, but does not yet have the verbal skills necessary to communicate how he feels or what he really wants.

* A desire to become more independent – this leads a toddler to attempt physical tasks beyond his capabilities.

* Being forced to eat just one more spoonful to satisfy the parent's perception of what he needs – a toddler will eat exactly the amount he needs to satisfy his hunger.

* Being over-stimulated and therefore becoming easily bored – a child who has too many new toys, watches too many DVDs or attends too many activity classes ceases to use his imagination and quickly becomes bored if he is not entertained the whole time. Boredom quickly turns into frustration if his demands to be entertained are not met immediately.

* Lengthy shopping trips – these nearly always end in tears. If possible, arrange for a friend with a toddler to watch both children for a couple of hours while you do your big shop. This favour can be reciprocated later.

* Overuse of the word 'no' – this can result in it not having the desired effect when you really do mean it. Think twice before using the word 'no'.

* Inconsistent parenting – both parents should work by the same set of rules, otherwise the toddler will become confused as to what is and is not acceptable behaviour.

Having a second baby – age gap

In the past I have written that there is no perfect age gap between children, and most families, when asked, will feel that the gap they chose is perfect for them. A gap of between 18 months and two years is quite common, but while having children reasonably close together may have benefits in the long term, it can create parenting challenges in the short term. The point at which the new baby is born coincides with the time the toddler is learning many different new skills, such as talking, potty training and getting dressed – all major hurdles that can cause a great deal of frustration for the toddler. A mother coping with a new baby may not have the time and patience to give the toddler the encouragement he needs at this important time, and the toddler will quickly pick up on his mother's tension. A mixture of the toddler's frustration and the mother's tension creates a ripe ground for tantrums.

With this 18-month to two-year age gap, getting the baby into a good routine is paramount, as it will give you the time you need to help your toddler cope with learning new skills. It is very important that your toddler realises you love him just as much as before the baby came along and that during each day there are still little slots of time that are just for you and him. Ensuring that he has learned as many of the skills as possible for his age and encouraging a certain amount of independence before the baby arrives will also help this phase go more smoothly.

The following chapters outline the various methods parents and carers can use to deal with tantrums, from positive praise and prevention to mild punishment or sanctions for consistently unwanted behaviour.

2
Dealing with Tantrums

Being aware of the main causes of toddler tantrums can help a parent to see a tantrum brewing and stop it before the matter gets out of hand – and before it becomes a serious habit. When feelings of anger, jealousy, fear and frustration get too much, there is bound to be a tantrum, as this is the way a toddler expresses his inner turmoil. It is really important to remember that your child is neither trying to annoy you nor being deliberately naughty, and that a positive approach is consistently more effective than punishment. How to deal with the situation depends very much on your child's age and the reason for the tantrum, but it is important that you remain consistent and calm, no matter how emotional the situation has become.

I do find that much of the so-called disobedience and bad behaviour of young children is caused by parents sending out confusing signals. The following are my suggestions for improving your child's behaviour:

* Psychologist Rudolf Dreikurs said, 'Children need encouragement, just as plants need water. They cannot survive without it.' He believed that encouragement is one of the most important skills a parent can learn in helping their children. Try always to accentuate the positive and eliminate the negative by praising your child's

strengths rather than commenting on his weaknesses. Expressing how pleased you are when he behaves well and reminding him of past times when he behaved well will do more to encourage good behaviour than reminding him of the times when he misbehaved.

✿ Grandparents who indulge children with presents and special treats are one thing, but on matters such as behaviour and manners they should follow your rules, otherwise it will only lead to your child becoming confused and to conflict within the family. A happy, relaxed family environment with a clear set of bound-aries is more likely to result in a confident, well-behaved child than an environment that is filled with mixed messages that result in tension and conflict.

✿ Keeping to a fixed bedtime and routine will help to avoid a lack of co-operation. It is often inconsistency over rules and limits that confuses a child of less than three years and results in bad behaviour. I would advise sticking to set mealtimes and avoiding later bedtimes.

* Make sure that the rules and limits you are setting are appropriate for your child's age, and avoid having too many of them. Concentrate on obtaining your child's co-operation on important matters such as getting ready for bed, getting dressed, holding your hand in the street, etc. Avoid rules that involve your child sitting quietly for lengthy periods; for example, it is unfair to expect a child of less than three years of age to sit quietly through lengthy adult lunches. Likewise, a child of this age can be encouraged to help tidy his toys and clothes away, but he is too young to be expected always to take the initiative to do so himself.

* Children learn very quickly, and if they are able to get away with bad behaviour in public they will use this to their advantage.

* Make sure your child has heard and understands your request properly. You should ensure that you have eye contact and that you have your child's full attention. Come down to their level if necessary.

* A child of over two years who is constantly in the buggy or car and not getting enough exercise and fresh air is more likely to be boisterous and noisy and get up to mischief around the home. All children benefit greatly from the opportunity to run around in the fresh air every day.

Dealing with tantrums in the second year

Listed below are guidelines that will help you deal with the tantrums your toddler may have in his second year.

Diversion

The majority of parents I know believe that diversion is one of the best methods of dealing with a tantrum. For distraction techniques to be effective you must get your toddler's attention at the beginning of the tantrum, before he has worked himself up into a frenzy. The following three distractions are the ones that I have found to be the most effective:

1 The majority of toddlers love playing with water, so get your toddler to wash some plastic containers or rinse the baby's bottles. If it is close to a mealtime, get him to help you wash some of the vegetables or fruit. On a warm day suggest that he helps you water the garden.

2 Keep a small selection of fun and safe toys for distraction – party hats, an inflated balloon, poppers or bubble liquid – and bring them out when you see that your toddler is getting tired and a tantrum is likely.

3 Keep a slab of ready-made pastry in the fridge and suggest a spot of baking when you notice your toddler is about to lose it. All the pounding and squeezing of the dough will soon get rid of excess frustration.

Removing your child from the situation

When distraction fails and your child is having a full-blown temper tantrum, try removing him from the situation. Placing him in his cot with the door shut for a short period of time is a particularly effective way of dealing with a toddler who decides to throw a tantrum in front of grandparents, relatives or friends, whose well-meaning interventions usually make matters worse.

Holding time

A small number of parents say that holding their toddler closely and firmly and talking to him in a soothing tone of voice until he calms down sometimes works. In my experience this can work only if he has not already worked himself up into a rage, if he is small and easy to grab hold of, or if he is sensitive and not very strong-willed.

Withdrawing attention

Some parents believe that the best way to deal with their toddler's tantrum is to let it run its course and totally ignore it. If necessary, go to another room so that the child realises he is no longer the centre of attention. I have occasionally seen this approach work but it has always been in families who are fortunate enough to have child-safe playrooms in full view of the kitchen. It may be worthwhile trying to ignore your child, but it is important that he is not left in a situation where he could harm himself.

Dealing with tantrums in the third year

During the second year, allowances are made for the toddler because he has no real concept of right or wrong. As the toddler enters his third year, however, nearly all parents expect some degree of obedience, and for many parents getting their toddler to do what he is told can become a real problem. Simple and reasonable requests such as 'clear your toys away', 'let's go upstairs for your bath' or 'take off your clothes' may all be met with total resistance, and a battle of wills between parent and toddler usually ends up with him in tears, accused of being naughty and disobedient.

All parents at some stage have to decide on appropriate

punishments for the times when their child has been deliberately disobedient. Parents who are in disagreement over standards of behaviour and forms of punishment send conflicting signals to their child as to what is acceptable and what isn't. In my experience, these parents usually end up with a very manipulative and spoilt child.

During the third year, the first step a child will take towards becoming more independent of his parents is to attend nursery school. A child who has not learned to co-operate with his parents at home will have a much more difficult time adapting to nursery school and taking instructions from other adults. All children will, from time to time, test their parents by being deliberately badly behaved, and some form of punishment may be needed.

When deciding on a suitable form of punishment, it is essential that the method you choose is appropriate. For example, when a child throws his food on the floor or scribbles on the wall, it would be better to make him clean the mess up than to make him take time out. Likewise, the child who loses his temper and throws his toys around should have the toys in question taken away for a short period. It is also important that the child is given a warning of the consequences if he should continue to misbehave. A firm verbal warning given properly and in the right manner can often eliminate the need for any further punishment.

Smacking

Thirty years ago a smack was considered a fairy normal way of dealing with a disobedient child. Smacking is still currently legal throughout the UK, but childcare experts and parents are divided on whether it is an effective way of dealing with bad behaviour. The current legal guidelines for smacking are that it must amount to 'reasonable punishment', but what is reasonable depends on the nature of the smack. It is considered unreasonable to cause a visible bruise, graze, scratch, swelling, mark or cut or to hit a child with an implement. Many child psychologists believe that smacking a child leads him to believe that violence is the way to deal with situations he can't control.

In my experience, the majority of parents who resort to smacking their child do so when they feel they are losing control of a situation and their temper snaps.

Only a very few of my clients have ever resorted to smacking as a regular form of punishment for their children, and it is my belief that as a punishment it rarely worked and only caused the children to behave more aggressively. I believe that there are other methods of sanctioning a child, as outlined in the following pages, that are far more effective than smacking.

Verbal warning

When giving your child a verbal warning, it is essential to have his undivided attention. If he tries to run away from you, it is important to restrain him by sitting him down in a chair and holding his hands while you explain why you are unhappy with him. With children under 36 months it is essential to keep explanations simple. All too often, I hear parents getting more and more fraught as they get trapped into lengthy discussions with very young children about why something isn't acceptable. If the behaviour is dangerous, then it certainly should be explained to the child why it might cause harm to him or others, but for misdemeanours such as jumping on the furniture or throwing books or clothes on the floor, saying something like 'Mummy doesn't do that, Daddy doesn't do that and Tommy mustn't do that' will suffice. Try to avoid statements like 'Tommy is naughty and he mustn't do that.'

The tone of your voice and facial expression will play a huge part in whether the warning is effective. All too often I hear reprimands sounding more like requests, which have little or no effect on the misbehaving child. I believe that without resorting to shouting you do need to raise your voice slightly, using the tone, along with the look in your eyes, to reflect how unhappy you are with your child's behaviour. A child must learn the consequences of his bad behaviour and it is important that a verbal warning does not turn into an empty threat. A child who is constantly threatened soon learns that his parents have no intention of punishing him and will become even more disobedient. If, despite giving your child a very firm warning, he continues to misbehave, the appropriate punishment should be administered immediately. Delaying the punishment for something he did several hours previously will only confuse him, as children under three years of age have not yet grasped the concept of time. Once he has been punished, the bad behaviour and punishment should not be mentioned again. Constantly reminding a child of his bad behaviour and using words such as 'naughty', 'nasty', 'clumsy', 'stupid' or 'silly' will not improve his behaviour – these words can in fact lead a child to have negative feelings about himself that cause him to be even more rebellious.

When a verbal reprimand does not have the desired effect, the two most effective punishments to choose from are either time out or withdrawal of a privilege. Which approach you take will depend very much on the age of your child and the reason for the bad behaviour.

Time out

In my experience, a short spell of time out is the most effective way of dealing with misbehaviour. Children under three love to be on the move the whole time and in the company of others, which is why a short spell of solitude is the quickest way to calm down a child whose behaviour is getting out of control. It also teaches a child the consequences of breaking the rules and that he must take responsibility for his own actions.

Childcare experts are in disagreement as to where time out should take place. Many advise against using the bedroom in case the child comes to associate this room with punishment and fear, which could consequently cause sleep problems. The 'naughty step' or 'naughty corner' are often suggested as alternatives. In my experience this rarely works (see the section that follows on page 43), and I agree with Dr Christopher Green that the bedroom is the best place for time out. As he points out in his book *Toddler Taming*, 'If putting a toddler in his bedroom will put him off sleeping, then presumably putting him in the bathroom will put him off washing, the dining room off eating, the sitting room off sitting, the kitchen off eating and so on. I choose the bedroom because it is sufficiently soundproof and far enough away from the rest of the living area to give both parties the space they need to calm down.'

A disobedient child who ignores a verbal warning should be taken to his bedroom immediately before things get totally out of control. Having decided on this course of action, it is essential that you carry it out quickly and calmly. The child who protests and screams should, if necessary, be picked up and carried there. The sooner you get your child to his room and leave him there, the quicker he will calm down and the less likely you will be to lose control of yourself and resort to shouting, arguing or nagging, which is what usually happens when parents keep trying to reason with a distraught and disobedient child.

The purpose of time out is to give your child the opportunity to calm down and realise how much more pleasurable life is when spent in the company of others and that bad behaviour in the company of others is not tolerated. Leaving him alone and reminding him that you will return the minute he has calmed down is the quickest way to achieve this. I do not think there is any great benefit in leaving a small child upset and alone for lengthy periods, as it usually results in the child becoming hysterical and trashing the room. I would allow a period of between three and five minutes, and if he hadn't calmed down I would return to the room and remind him that he would be allowed out if he was ready to behave. The answer is nearly always 'yes'.

Therefore I would ask him for an apology and a cuddle, then bring him out. However, should he start misbehaving again I would repeat the whole procedure. With some children the procedure has to be repeated many, many times, but eventually they learn that an ignored warning of bad behaviour will always result in them being taken to their room.

The Naughty Step

Every parenting conversation I've had recently seems to bring up the subject of young children's behaviour and, specifically, 'the naughty step'. I've been asked for my views on this method of discipline and, having seen it used on many occasions, I hope the following might help anyone who is considering putting this method into practice.

The principle of 'the naughty step' seems to be the modern equivalent of being sent to your bedroom. The way it works is that, when a child behaves in an unacceptable way, he is encouraged to sit on the step in silence until he has calmed down, at which point he is permitted to return to the rest of the family. The theory is that this gives the child valuable time out and defuses the tension for everyone else. The long-term use of this method means that you can threaten the naughty step the next time the child misbehaves, and in theory they will then do as they are told to avoid being put on it again.

Sometimes it works a treat; there are occasions where a child so hates being moved away from everyone else that he quickly learns the rules of behaviour and things improve for the parents. However, I have often been looking after a baby in a household where the nanny caring for the older children has been trying to use the naughty step. This is usually because the parents are keen on its use. These poor nannies often find themselves chasing the children round the house trying to get them on to the step. The initial misdemeanour is completely forgotten, as everyone gets upset trying either to implement or avoid the naughty step discipline.

If you decide to adopt this method, there are a few questions worth considering in advance:

* At what age can you try using it?

* What sort of behaviour do you use it for?

* What do you do if the child won't sit on it?

* What do you do if the child's behaviour doesn't improve, regardless of the naughty step threat?

* What alternatives are there?

In my view, the naughty step can only be used for children aged between about two and a half and five years. By the age of two and a half most children should be capable of following simple instructions. Once a child is five and in full-time school there is a whole new set of rules, and home needs to be a safe and secure place for him to relax after the demands of a school day.

I have recently spoken to a few parents who were trying to use the naughty step when their child wouldn't eat (more of this later). Other parents have told me that they use it when a child breaks or damages something, but that their partners use it to punish rudeness. This sums up one of the main problems of this particular punishment – incon-sistency. Use of the naughty step needs to be absolutely consistent. If you want to try it, you, your partner and your children need to sit down and discuss the issue together. Is it a punishment for violence towards a sibling or other child? Is it for damage to toys or other household items? Is it for disobedience? Or what about rudeness? If you are not *all* clear what *all* the rules are, then it will never work as a deterrent. Nor will you see an improvement in your child's behaviour if one day he is put on the step for writing on the wall, but the next day daddy lets him off after he breaks a sibling's toy. You will simply end up confusing and upsetting your child and getting frustrated.

Nor can you depend entirely on the naughty step to discipline your child because its use is limited to your own home. There is no equivalent when you are out and about or at a friend's house. There will be children who work this out and take advantage of being in a public place to throw a tantrum. Also, many mothers tell me that behaviour that might not bother them one day drives them crazy the next. This is perfectly understandable – mothers today are under tremendous pressure, frequently trying to manage children, homes and jobs. But it sends very confusing messages to your children if the use of the naughty step is dependent upon how you are feeling at that particular time.

There are some children who will go straight to the step for their time out when their parents ask them. But in the majority of cases I have witnessed, the child is being disobedient in the first place, so resists going to the step when requested. This results in the parents become angrier and the sanctions escalating as the resistance becomes more embedded. Five minutes on the naughty step soon turns into 10 minutes in a room by themselves, confiscation of a favourite toy, cancellation of a forthcoming treat, no television for a day, and so on. A minor misdemeanour can escalate into a major crime, and parents feel desperate to take back control.

I appreciate that what the vast majority of parents are trying to do is teach their children how to behave in order that home life is peaceful, relaxing and fun for everyone, but, over and above any practical issues, my main problem with the naughty step is the fundamental message of punishment that it sends to the child. It simply doesn't allow any room for rewarding good behaviour. It is an essentially negative way of dealing with your children. Put yourself in the place of your child and imagine that you have had a bad day at work. You are tired and hungry and don't feel like doing much. Your husband comes home and you are short-tempered with him. Instead of trying to understand why you are not feeling cheerful and relaxed, your husband insists you sit by yourself in a corner until you are able to be nice again. Children under five are not able to explain why they feel the way they do. They have no sense of how their feelings affect their behaviour, but those feelings are there regardless.

Withdrawal of privileges

A simplified version of withdrawal of privileges can be used as a child approaches his third birthday, but because a child of this age still does not have much awareness of time, the withdrawal of privileges must happen immediately. A child who is deliberately being destructive with a toy or book, or who scribbles all over the kitchen table, should have the item in question removed for the remainder of the day. Likewise, the child who insists on running around while eating a biscuit should have the biscuit taken away, and the child who misbehaves at a play date can be taken home. However, not allowing your child to watch a DVD in the evening or cancelling a trip to the playground in the afternoon because he misbehaved in the morning will not be effective.

As with time out, the child should always be given a verbal warning of what will happen if he continues to misbehave. If you find you constantly have to reprimand or punish your child for deliberate misbehaviour, it is essential to look closely at both the reasons for the misbehaviour and the forms of punishment you are using. It is also worthwhile discussing any worries you may have about your child's behaviour with your health visitor, who will be able to reassure you as to whether or not your concerns have any foundation.

Finding the right method

We all know that babies and young children need to be guided by their parents into learning the right ways to behave. The 'right' way is frequently the socially acceptable way (don't bite or hit anyone; say please and thank you); often it is the safe way (stop at the edge of the road; don't touch the hot oven door); sometimes it is our own definition of manners (try not to interrupt when I am talking; eat what is on your plate). Instilling good behaviour into children is a never-ending and ongoing process. It's not going to happen overnight, it needs perseverance and consistency, and there really aren't any shortcuts or quick fixes.

The final choice as to whether you use any method of punishment for your children's behaviour is down to you and your partner. Every child is different and you should try to find an approach to discipline that suits your child's temperament. The more suitable it is, the easier and more effective it will be. In my experience the majority of children respond far better to positive praise and reinforcement of good behaviour than they ever do to negativity and being told that they are 'naughty' or, even worse, 'bad'. A good tip is to try to think in terms of your child's 'behaviour' being appropriate or inappropriate, rather than your actual child being good or otherwise. Like all of us, children get tired and cranky, but in general they want to please. So, focus on their positive behaviour, rewarding them with plenty of attention and praise, and where possible play down any inappropriate behaviour. It's a simple message, but in my experience it has a powerful effect.

The importance of positive praise

My preferred approach has always been to positively reinforce the good behaviour, not to highlight the bad. I don't even like to use the word 'naughty' with a child. When I have cared for older children I have found they respond far more effectively and quickly when they are praised and encouraged for what they do well. I'm a big fan of a parenting technique called descriptive praise. This is where you praise a child by describing to them exactly what it is that you think they have done well. For example:

* 'It was really great how you helped to tidy up the toys just then.'

* 'You sat so nicely with your toys while mummy fed the baby. Thank you.'

* 'Thank you for asking to leave the table; what lovely manners you have.'

* 'Granny thought you were very good at saying please and thank you.'

* 'That was very clever of you to wait for me by the road.'

Experts advise that parents try to say five positive things like this to their children before breakfast! They suggest that you praise your children not just for doing things right, but also for not doing them wrong: for example, 'That was great how you managed to get one sock on by yourself today.'

If you have never tried this with your child, it might feel a bit silly at first as you go over the top in your enthusing, but you should notice a dramatic improvement in behaviour. Think back to that occasion when you snapped at your partner for leaving his shoes in the middle of the hallway. Instead of sending you to your room, he told you how hard he realises you have been working recently and how much he appreciates the efforts you make at home. Your temper vanished. You probably picked his shoes up yourself. The point is that we all respond better to positivity. We all like to feel that our efforts are noticed and valued, however small.

Another point that may seem obvious is to take the time to explain things to children, rather than just saying 'no'. All mothers are under pressure at times and sometimes expect too much from their children, but even very young children can understand a simple explanation of why the hot tap shouldn't be touched or why it isn't a good idea to run across the road. When your child is older you might find you get a lot more co-operation when you explain why it isn't possible to go somewhere at a particular time or why a friend can't come over to play that day. Empathise with your child's feelings of disappointment or frustration and discuss alternative plans if appropriate. Being on the same side as your child can go a long way to avoiding conflict; and the channels of communication that open between you now will stand you in good stead when your little baby becomes a great big teenager!

As well as praising your children for good behaviour, you could try using star charts. I have found these very effective for solving specific problems. If it's driving you mad that toys aren't tidied away when you ask, or that the toilet isn't being flushed after use, introduce a star chart for encouragement. A row or a whole card full of stars can mean a treat, such as a toy or a special trip, but try not to use sweets or food as a reward.

Head-banging and breath-holding

Some toddlers are prone to holding their breath or banging their heads against the floor or other surfaces during tantrums. Such episodes are usually short-lived, but can be very upsetting for parents. If you are concerned about this then do seek advice and reassurance from your health visitor or GP.

3
Learning New Skills

A child has so much to learn during the toddler years when in a very short space of time he changes from a baby into someone who can walk, talk and feed himself. A toddler absorbs huge amounts of information every day, but it takes him time to learn and this can be a constant source of frustration.

Imagine how it would feel to be able to understand

everything that people were saying around you, but not to have the vocabulary to express your own thoughts and desires; to be able to see how to do things, but to be incapable of doing them for yourself. What appears to be bad behaviour from a toddler is often just his way of communicating the frustrations he feels at his own limitations.

Bear in mind the following:

* By the time your child is two he will be more physically able as his walking becomes steadier and he learns to run, climb and jump. It is, however, important to recognise that he faces many new challenges and can still be frustrated by the things he cannot yet achieve.

* As your toddler becomes more physically adventurous, try not to hover over him anxiously as he learns new skills. If you are very overprotective, your child will start

to feel your anxiety. This can make him lose his natural instinct to explore and the courage that enables him to try new things.

* Remember that we learn by our mistakes. Parents who are constantly pushing their children to succeed in everything they do, for example who correct attempts at colouring or doing puzzles in order to make them appealing to an adult eye, will end up making their child anxious and frightened of disapproval. This can leave a child feeling unhappy and frustrated at what he perceives as his own inability to please and can be a catalyst for bad behaviour.

* When your child is learning to feed and dress himself, it will take time. You will need to allow for this, and don't expect him to get things done in the time that you would take to do things for him. If he is allowed to go at his

own pace he will learn but you will need to be patient and encouraging. It may be quicker and easier to do things for him, but this will only build frustrations in the long run as he will not be able to do things for himself.

* When you are trying to teach your child to do something new, choose your time carefully. If you decide to teach him a new skill just before teatime when he is tired and hungry, it is likely to end in frustration and tantrums.

* It is important to recognise that your child will take time to learn new skills. Praise him for his attempts at getting dressed or putting things away, even if they aren't done exactly as you would like!

* Never undermine your child's attempts at learning new skills by comparing him to others of the same age. This will be very dispiriting for him. Every child is different

and some will do certain things more quickly and skilfully than others. Children who have an older brother or sister often learn more quickly as they copy their sibling. Constant criticism and comparison will not encourage a toddler to behave well.

✿ When children are concentrating hard on learning a new skill, they can get very angry if they can't do what they want. When parents step in to help, this can sometimes exacerbate the situation. It may be better to try to focus your toddler's attention on something else by offering him a drink or a snack, to give him time to calm down and relax.

✿ Always try to accentuate the positive when your child is learning new skills, as encouragement is often the best way to help a child who is misbehaving because he can't achieve something.

✿ Sometimes disobedience can be the result of overconfidence in children who are aware of their increasing independence. It is important to get the balance right with praise so that your child develops a healthy sense of self-esteem, but doesn't end up feeling that what he wants is the only thing that matters.

Walking

While the majority of toddlers are walking soon after their first birthday, it can take several more months of practice to achieve the balance and co-ordination needed for steady walking. Until this is achieved toddlers do not have the ability to steer themselves properly. During this stage there will be much falling over and bumping into things, which can lead to frustration and tantrums.

Listed below are suggestions and guidelines that will

help to make things easier for your toddler during the early stages of walking:

* Toddlers find it easier to walk if they go barefoot, as splaying their toes helps them get a better grip. It is also better for muscle tone and the development of their feet. In very cold weather it is preferable for your toddler to wear socks with non-slip soles when he is walking indoors; even the softest shoes can restrict his growth.

* The first toddling steps are often referred to as 'cruising'. A toddler will begin by walking sideways first. He uses both hands to pull himself up and hold on to the furniture and support himself as he moves around. Arrange sturdy furniture closer together to encourage cruising.

* As his balance improves, he begins to use only one hand on the furniture for support. Eventually he becomes

confident enough to take a couple of unsupported steps between any small gaps in the furniture.

* As his confidence grows, he relies less and less on the furniture for support, moving farther and farther away from it. Eventually he takes three or four unsupported steps forward at a time.

* Once he is capable of taking a few steps forward, a push-along toy can help him learn to balance. At first he will be unable to control the speed, so it is important always to supervise him, otherwise he will tend to fall flat as it gets away from him.

* Avoid using the round type of baby walker on wheels. They are responsible for 5,000 accidents a year. The Chartered Society of Physiotherapists claims they may also hinder physical and mental development.

✿ Once your toddler has been walking properly for about six weeks, a qualified fitter should measure him for his first pair of shoes. It is important to invest in a pair of shoes that are both the right length and the right width. Shoes that do not support his feet properly could cause permanent damage.

Talking

The sooner a toddler is able to communicate his needs by talking, the easier it becomes for parents to control frustration and tantrums. Children learn to talk by listening, and, while it makes sense to spend lots of time talking to your toddler, it is very important that you also give him the opportunity to respond to what you are saying. Communication is a two-way thing and should be fun for your toddler. Although you may not understand much of what he is saying, by showing him you are really interested in his attempts at talking you will encourage him to talk even more.

Speech varies greatly from toddler to toddler; as a guideline:

* By 15 months most toddlers are able to say between six and eight words.

* By 18 months most toddlers are able to say between 20 and 40 words.

* At two years of age most toddlers are able to string two words together – for example, 'more juice' and 'mummy gone'.

* By the time they reach two and a half years, most will have a vocabulary of about 200 words.

If you have any worries or concerns about your child's speech development, it is advisable to seek advice from your health visitor or GP.

The following guidelines will help encourage your toddler to become a confident talker:

* Reading to your child is an excellent way of increasing his vocabulary. Try to spend at least two short quiet spells a day reading to your toddler, pointing at things in pictures as you do so. While you are reading, avoid other distractions such as answering the telephone or having the television or radio playing in the background.

* Make sure you speak slowly and clearly so that your child is able to see your mouth movements as you pronounce the words. Keep sentences short and simple until about the end of the second year. Once your toddler

is stringing three or four words together himself, you can lengthen your sentences.

* Do not correct your toddler when he pronounces a word incorrectly as this will only discourage his attempts at talking. Instead, it is better to say the word correctly when you answer him.

* All toddlers love to mimic adults, so singing nursery rhymes that involve lots of exaggerated facial expressions along with the constant repetition of certain words is a great way to help your toddler's verbal skills.

* Discuss things you are doing with your toddler, and emphasise the key words in your sentence. Avoid using pronouns such as 'your' or 'it', and use your child's name, for example, 'Let's put on Jack's red shoes,' or 'Where is Jack's blue ball?'

* It is worth making a list of any new words you notice your toddler using, and making sure that they are introduced as much as possible into conversations you and the rest of the family have with him.

* Finally, as your toddler's vocabulary increases, be prepared to repeat yourself over and over again as he constantly asks the same questions. This is all part of your child learning how to talk, and the more patient you are when answering his questions the more eager he will be to communicate.

Dressing

By the age of 14 months most toddlers have learned how to pull off their hat and socks. This is an excellent time to introduce activity toys that will help your toddler develop his manipulation skills. Shape-sorter toys, and dolls that have a variety of fastenings, such as zips, toggles and buttons, will all help him do this. It is important to allow lots of extra time while your toddler is learning this skill. He will need lots of encouragement, and will quickly sense if you are in a hurry and becoming impatient.

The following guidelines will help your toddler learn to dress and undress himself:

* Between 18 and 24 months the majority of toddlers will be able to remove most of their clothes, and by 30 months most are capable of getting totally undressed and dressed, but they will need help with buttons, poppers and buckles.

* Your toddler will be less likely to get frustrated or bored if you teach him to undress and dress in stages. Once

he is capable of taking off his socks and trousers, move on to him taking off his socks, trousers and pants, etc. Use the same approach when teaching him how to dress himself.

✿ Encourage his independence by allowing him some choice in what he wears, but do limit the choice so that you remain in control.

4

Food Fights

Having a meal together should be a happy time for the family to enjoy together, but it can easily turn into a source of huge anxiety for both parents and children. It's a familiar scene to many parents who will have spent time cooking nutritious food only to find a delicious meal is met with stubborn refusal; or who have spent time coaxing, cajoling or even bribing a child to eat to find that lunch still goes untouched straight into the bin. What often begins as a small issue over eating a particular food can quickly escalate and lead to stressed parents and a child who has regular mealtime tantrums.

This may spring from the desire to do the best for a child by ensuring he eats a healthy, balanced diet, but trying to enforce good eating habits in the wrong way can exacerbate the problem. Once parents have begun to get stressed at mealtimes, this will be picked up by a child who will sit down for each meal feeling tense and ready for a fight. Tantrums at mealtimes can upset the whole family, and that's why it's so important to get to the root of the problem quickly so that everyone can enjoy family mealtimes again.

Few things annoy parents as much as fussy children who turn up their noses at perfectly good food. I know that mothers can be driven to the point of tears when, at the end of a long day, their carefully prepared meal ends up in the bin or the dog. But there is nothing more likely to stop a child from eating than tension and anxiety. I advise parents never to argue with a child about eating what is on his plate. It simply results in everyone getting upset. Instead, make it clear there is no alternative and remove the food immediately. I have watched parents cajole children into eating, bribe them with puddings and threaten them with punishments if they don't eat. None of these is the ideal way to approach fussy eating, and the threat of a punishment is more likely to physically prevent a child from eating as he becomes tense and upset. Could you eat a plate of food after someone had threatened you? With eating disorders and problems of obesity among children on the increase, parents generally need to be very careful what messages they attach to food and eating.

Here are some useful guidelines:

* Try to stick to set mealtimes whenever you possibly can. Young children know where they are with a regular

routine, and it will help avoid some of the eating problems that can arise.

* Be realistic about how long you expect your child to sit quietly at the table during mealtimes. Of course, you should expect him to sit and eat his own meal properly, but it is unfair to expect a toddler to stay at the table during a long adult lunch. Let him get down from the table once he has finished eating.

* Children who fuss at mealtimes are often not really hungry. If your child is eating too much between meals, or drinks a lot just before a meal, he is less likely to eat well at mealtimes and this can lead to battles.

* Never try to force-feed a toddler who is refusing to eat as this will almost inevitably lead to tears and will make mealtimes a source of anxiety for parents and their

child. If a child is not hungry, there is no point in forcing food on him, but it is important not to start offering biscuits or puddings as an alternative if a child won't touch his meal.

* Sometimes parents expect toddlers to eat unrealistic quantities of food. Offering small quantities and then giving more if a child is still hungry is better than piling a plate high with food, which can be daunting.

* Try not to give in to coaxing or bribing a child to eat. It is far better to leave him peacefully with a plate of food. If a child is used to being offered treats if he eats, he will learn to expect this.

* Remember that children learn by observation. The best way to encourage good behaviour and table manners is to set a good example. If you don't sit down at the

table and eat a meal but instead resort to snacking while dashing about, you can't expect your child to sit at a table and eat peacefully.

❀ As your child learns to feed himself, some spills and mess are inevitable. Don't constantly reprimand him for less than immaculate table manners as this can lead to anxiety. By the time your child is three he should be able to eat without making too much mess. If your expectations are realistic, you are less likely to encounter bad behaviour.

A toddler's appetite

During the first year, babies grow rapidly. Most babies will have increased their height by 50 per cent and trebled their birth weight by the time they reach their first birthday. In the second year, growth slows down and there is often a very noticeable decrease in a toddler's appetite. Unfortunately many parents are not aware that the decrease in their toddler's appetite is normal. They become anxious that he is not eating enough and often resort to spoon-feeding him in the vain hope that it will get his old appetite back. The pressure to get the toddler to eat more usually has the opposite effect and results in what many childcare experts term 'food fights'. Mealtimes soon become a battleground, with the toddler screaming as his parents insist on him having just one more spoonful. If you wish to avoid these feeding problems with your toddler, or if he is already experiencing them, it is essential that you have a clear understanding of what he needs to eat for a healthy and well-balanced diet. This will help avoid food fights and fussy eating and will also encourage long-term healthy eating habits. See *The Contented Child's Food*

Bible for more information on portion sizes and recommended daily amounts.

A toddler who is still drinking from a bottle and continues to be given lots of puréed and mashed foods during the second year will be much slower to learn self-feeding. To help develop the pincer-grip (forefinger and thumb grasp) necessary for confident self-feeding, it is essential to introduce lots of finger foods and chopped fruit and vegetables. Feeding bottles should be replaced with a non-spill type of beaker by the age of one year.

The following guidelines will help your toddler learn how to feed himself:

❁ Between 12 and 15 months most toddlers will attempt to use a spoon, although they will need help with loading it and directing it into their mouth.

* By 18 months a toddler who has had enough practice will manage to eat most of his food by himself using a spoon. Self-feeding with a spoon will be made easier for a toddler if the food is in a bowl.

* At two years of age a toddler should have developed enough hand–eye co-ordination to eat his food with a small fork and should manage to eat all of his meal without assistance. Toddlers will learn to use cutlery sooner if they are allowed to join in some family meals and encouraged to copy the adults.

What if things are really bad and you are at your wits' end? You have tried everything you can think of, but your child simply refuses to eat certain foods. All your friends tell you to relax and that he will grow out of it, but you just can't when all he will eat is breadsticks and cheese.

By this stage your child's behaviour and your responses are deeply ingrained. This problem has probably been around for quite a while, perhaps even years. If your child is healthy and well apart from this problem, it is likely that you need to make some change in your own behaviour and the way you handle this situation.

First, however, it is important to have your child medically examined to make sure there are no underlying medical reasons for his fussiness, and also to make sure that he is healthy. Explain your concerns to your GP. Ask for blood tests to check your child's iron levels and have him weighed and measured to make sure he is growing properly. Second, if your child has not eaten a balanced or varied diet for a while, it may be advisable to start a vitamin and mineral supplement until his diet has improved. Once you are reassured that he is well, it is time to start the following strategy.

Ending the battle

Stress is an appetite-killer for many people, including children. When your child sits down at the table to eat and knows from experience that a battle is about to begin, his stress level automatically rises. The body releases hormones that reduce the blood supply to the stomach and other areas, and appetite is reduced. Obviously, starting a meal in this condition is not conducive to healthy eating, so you need to call a truce. Of course, don't say this to your child – you don't want to alert him to your secret plan! Children are often too immature to understand the complexities of the situation they are in, so it is up to you to be cunning and consistent. Any inconsistencies in your behaviour will trigger doubt in your child's mind, and the situation will not improve.

Also it is crucial that both parents are on the same wavelength. There is nothing more confusing and destructive to a child than having two parents who give conflicting information: the child will soon see one parent as 'good' and another as 'bad'. If siblings are old enough to understand, explain what you are doing and why. If they are young, simply treat them in exactly the same way as the fussy eater.

Try this step-by-step strategy:

* **Step 1** – Begin by restoring peace once again to your mealtimes. Start by eliminating the main behaviour that leads to arguments and stress in both the parent and the child. As the most common area of concern for parents with fussy eaters is the lack of vegetables in the diet, we will use this as our example, but the following advice can be applied to any type of food.

Let's say you serve vegetables to your child every evening and he refuses to eat them. Begin the strategy by simply not feeding him any vegetables. If he requests certain ones, serve only these and praise him for eating them as well as the rest of the meal. Meanwhile, continue to prepare your usual vegetables for the rest of the family, but do not serve any to the fussy eater. Expect him to feel quite elated by your behaviour and possibly also feel that he has won the 'battle'. Do not discuss your motives or anything related to the issue: just do not serve the vegetables, and act as if nothing has happened. Try to let go of the stress you normally experience at mealtimes: simply feel relieved that there is nothing to argue about.

Continue this new behaviour for one to two weeks. Once the problem is removed your child will very quickly forget and should be more relaxed. With any luck you will too, and mealtimes will be a lot more enjoyable. You will no doubt be concerned that your child does not eat vegetables, but do not let this show.

✿ **Step 2** – Now it's time to start the second part of the strategy. When shopping, look for a vegetable that you like but that you know your child has never eaten or even seen before. Starting with something sweet is usually a good idea, so try a sweet potato or butternut squash. Both can be baked in the oven, whole or sliced. Serve it at the table with the rest of the meal. Do not offer your child any and have a general conversation about the vegetable. Talk about where it comes from, where it grows – under the ground or on a tree – what the shape reminds you of, what the colour resembles, anything to make the vegetable sound intriguing. You could do an Internet search to gather some interesting information to discuss at the table. Children have vivid imaginations, and if you can trigger their curiosity they are more likely to try something new.

Do not expect your child to try the new vegetable the first time it appears, but continue to introduce new vegetables, or simply prepare familiar ones in different ways. Never offer your child some, or even suggest he tries it, because this will no doubt have the opposite effect. Eventually most children will ask to taste some.

If your child won't eat any cooked vegetables, offer them raw, as crudités, which children often prefer. Cut them into bite-sized pieces and serve with a familiar dip, such as salsa, hummus, cream cheese or mayonnaise. Simply place them on the dining table, or on a table in a room where you know he will spend some time, and see what happens **(of course, never leave your child unattended when he is eating).** If unsuccessful, try again when your child's friend comes to visit. Often the friend will tuck in, and your child will follow suit!

5

Bedtime Battles

Bedtime is not always the calm event that we like to imagine, with a cheerful but sleepy toddler settling down for a story before falling peacefully asleep. Attempting to get an unwilling toddler into bed can turn into a battle of wills that ends in deadlock with a child who is too upset and angry to sleep. Sometimes it can be lack of sleep that has created the problem in the first place as overtiredness is one of the most common causes of toddler tantrums.

The importance of a routine

Having a familiar routine with a set bedtime will certainly help to make this a less fraught time of day. Here are some useful guidelines:

* A lack of sleep can make a child more prone to anger and aggression. When a child who is usually calm at bedtime starts having problems on a regular basis, a slightly earlier bedtime is often the solution.

* If your toddler has just started going to a nursery or playgroup, he will be very tired at first, and this often causes bedtime battles. You may find that you need to bring forward his bedtime a little.

* A late bedtime is often the cause of bad behaviour in toddlers. At this age they need a good 11–12 hours of

sleep at night and perhaps also a nap of one or two hours in the daytime. Any less than this can make them more prone to misbehaviour.

* Make sure you have a fixed bedtime and routine. Inconsistency is confusing to a small child and this can result in bad behaviour. Both parents should follow the same bedtime routine as far as is possible. If a child knows that one parent will let them stay up later, this inconsistency will make getting him into bed and asleep far more difficult.

* Avoid boisterous games and activities just before bed as an excited child will find it difficult to settle and will be more likely to have bedtime tantrums.

* Toddlers often move from a cot to a bed at this age, and parents who have experienced perfectly calm bedtimes

may start to find things more difficult. This is a big change for a toddler, and some find it quite threatening, especially if it coincides with the arrival of a new baby. You may find it takes a few weeks to settle back into a bedtime routine.

* Toddlers sometimes develop what may seem to be irrational fears, becoming frightened of the dark or terrified of monsters at night. Don't dismiss this as it is a real fear for your child, however silly it may seem to you. Trying to get a frightened child to sleep will not be easy. You may want to leave a small plug-in nightlight in his room, or leave his bedroom door open so there is a dim source of light outside.

* If you have had battles getting your child to bed that have ended in tears and arguments, he is far more likely to wake up in the night. Keeping to a regular, calm bedtime routine will make this less likely.

Case study: Samantha, aged 28 months
Problem: Difficulty in settling to sleep
Cause: Overtiredness and fear of the dark

Samantha had never had a set bedtime routine and was never put in her own cot until her parents went to bed at around 11pm. She would often fall asleep during the early part of the evening on the living room sofa, but never more than 30–40 minutes at a time. She would then wake up at least twice in the night and have to be resettled back to sleep by her mother, usually by being cuddled or being given a drink of juice, and sometimes both. She would awaken at around 6am in the morning, ready to start the day. During the day she would have a couple of short naps usually lasting between 20 and 40 minutes, either in the car or in her buggy. She never went in her cot during the day, and her sleep in total over a 24-hour day was around nine hours, which is considerably less than a child of her age usually needs. When Samantha was just over two years old her mother went back to work part-time, which meant that Samantha started to go to nursery three days a week. She was dropped off at 8am in the morning by her father, then picked up in the evening by her mother at around 5pm.

Because Samantha had only ever been used to sleeping in the car or her buggy during the day, she would not settle down for a nap alongside the other children after lunch. By the time her mother picked her up in the evening she was totally exhausted and usually fell asleep during the 20-minute car journey home. Her mother, now working three days a week *as a carer in a residential home for the elderly, was also exhausted at the end of her nine-hour shift. She began to find it increasingly difficult to cope with Samantha's late bedtime and middle-of-the-night wakings and decided that an earlier bedtime for both her and Samantha was necessary if she was going to be able to cope with her demanding job. She believed that Samantha was a child who needed less sleep than the average recommendations and aimed to bring her bedtime forward to around 9pm. She had a bath and bedtime routine at around 8pm, in the hope that she could settle in her cot by 9pm.*

Unfortunately, because Samantha had only ever gone into her cot when she was absolutely exhausted, establishing an earlier bedtime and a routine proved much more difficult than her mother had imagined.

Samantha would scream and scream the minute she was put in her cot. Often she would get so hysterical that she would throw up. She continued to wake up in the night but started to take longer and longer to settle back to sleep, and even then would only do so if the bedroom door was left open and her light full on. After two weeks of trying to establish a routine using the sleep training method, things had got worse. Her mother rang me desperate for advice on how to establish a bedtime routine and improve on Samantha's night-time sleep.

I explained to her that Samantha's main problems were that she had learned all the wrong sleep associations. In addition she suffered from serious overtiredness, fighting sleep and being able to fall asleep only when absolutely exhausted. There was also the fact that she was used to sleeping on and off during the earlier part of her night in the sitting room, where there was always a light on. To expect her suddenly to settle in her cot by herself in a dark room was unrealistic at an age when even the best of sleepers start to experience all sorts of fears and anxieties. I advised that with Samantha the best way to resolve the problem would be to use the gradual withdrawal method. It could take several weeks to establish but in Samantha's case it would probably be more effective than sleep training.

I advised her mother to start Samantha's bedtime routine no later than 6pm and have her settled in her cot by 7pm. However, for the first few nights the light should be left low and she should stay in the room with her. I wanted to create the same atmosphere in her bedroom as she was used to in the sitting room during the early evening. Samantha could have toys in her cot and look at books, and listen to tapes on her cassette recorder. Her mother should potter around the room and sit in the chair reading a book, but everything should be kept very low-key, with talking kept to a minimum. When Samantha eventually fell asleep at around 11pm her mother could leave the room, and when she woke in the night her mother was to return, give her a quick drink and a cuddle to reassure her, but not talk at great length. She should remain in the room but sitting on the chair until Samantha fell back to sleep.

By the fifth night Samantha was adapting to her new evening routine and actually falling asleep much earlier, usually around 9.30pm. I advised her mother *that she should now install an even dimmer night-light and limit the toys and books in the room. She should also start to leave the room every 15 minutes for around one minute at a time, standing outside the door and reassuring Samantha that she would be back in a minute. The time should be extended by a further 30 seconds every 15 minutes until she reached a stage where she was leaving the room for five minutes every 15 minutes. The same procedure had to be followed in the night after she had been given a quick cuddle and a small drink. We continued this pattern for a further week, after which time I felt that Samantha was well used to the room, the bedtime routine and being in her cot from 7pm, and that we could try again with the sleep training method.*

On the first night of sleep training Samantha was

settled in her cot with two of her favourite toys and with a very low voltage night-light. Her mother kissed her goodnight at 7pm and turned on her music tape. Samantha started to protest but her mother quickly left the room and waited 10 minutes before she returned. On her return she stayed in the room only one or two minutes and reassured Samantha that she was only next door and that it was night-time and everyone had to be very quiet at night-time. She would then leave the room and wait a further 15 minutes before returning and going through the same procedure. After about 50 minutes Samantha fell asleep. When she woke two hours later her mother repeated the same procedure as before, but after first checking at 15 minutes she increased the time between visits to 20 minutes.

She continued the same procedure every night for over a week, but gradually increasing the time between the visits and decreasing the amount of reassurance she gave Samantha. A following week of sleep training got increasingly easier and some nights Samantha settled herself back before her mother was due to check her. By the end of the final week of sleep training Samantha was settling easily in her cot with her music, usually falling asleep between 7.15pm and 7.30pm.

She would usually sleep soundly until 6.00 or 6.30pm but would stay happily in her cot until 7am.

6
The Social Toddler

Children love to play and will enjoy time spent at play-groups or in the playground, but tantrums are very common when small children are playing together. Although they may seem to enjoy being together, toddlers are still learning social skills and it takes them time to learn to share with one another and to understand that at a certain time they will have to stop playing and go home.

It is important to recognise that what appears to an adult to be bad behaviour when toddlers are together is often just their lack of social skills. These are things that have to be learned, and when children are still learning they are extremely self-centred. Frustration and tantrums are inevitable as they learn.

Bear in mind the following guidelines:

* Toddlers can really benefit from attending a nursery or organised playgroup as it teaches them to join in with group activities and to share.

* If you can, try to introduce nursery or playgroup gradually. If a child is suddenly spending entire days constantly surrounded by other children, it can leave him feeling completely exhausted and will lead to bad behaviour and tantrums. If you can build up the number of days your child attends nursery gradually, he won't get so tired.

* A child who has not been taught how to co-operate with others will find it far more difficult to adapt to a nursery or playgroup as he will not be used to listening to adults and following instructions. This can also lead to problems with other children at nursery.

* Parents need to present a united front about what is and is not acceptable behaviour because sending out conflicting signals is confusing for a child. A lack of clear boundaries and disagreement between parents often results in a child who becomes manipulative and spoilt. For example, you both need to agree on what you consider to be acceptable behaviour in social play – how many of his toys should your toddler be expected to share when friends come to play, and is it reasonable if your child wants to keep some toys for himself?

* Toddlers can get very engrossed in their play, and if you expect them to stop suddenly because it is time for a meal or to go out they may feel angry and frustrated. Make sure you warn your child about five minutes in advance that it is nearly time to stop playing. Don't just shout at him from a distance, but go and talk to him directly and make sure he has understood what you have said.

* If your child loses his temper when he is playing and throws his toys around, taking the toys away for a while is often the most effective form of punishment.

Aggressive behaviour

The majority of toddlers will occasionally use some form of aggressive behaviour, such as hitting, kicking, biting or scratching. In my experience, toddlers who resort to this sort of aggressive behaviour usually do so when they are feeling insecure. Some feel resentful and jealous when they suddenly find they have to share their parents' attention with a new baby, or share the toys with other children at playgroup. A toddler who has not yet learned to share may try to retrieve his toy from another by kicking. The mother breast-feeding the new baby may be subjected to a sudden bite from a toddler who is feeling neglected. A gentle stroke of the baby's cheek by the toddler may end up as a very severe scratch. Although all of these spur-of-the-moment attacks are intentional, they are not planned and the toddler does not yet understand what causes him to make them. Unlike tantrums, which are usually directed only at parents, aggressive behaviour can often be directed at anyone who the toddler feels is a threat. The toddler who gets into the habit of using aggressive behaviour as a way of asserting himself or of getting undivided attention will quickly become very unpopular with other parents and children.

To deal with aggressive behaviour, follow these guidelines:

* A toddler must learn that aggressive behaviour in any form is not acceptable. Therefore it is foolish to deal with this problem by smacking him or, even worse, as some books suggest, 'biting him back'.

* If your toddler lashes out aggressively in one way or another, immediately take him to one side and explain simply and firmly that biting, hitting, etc. is not allowed. Avoid using words like 'bad' or 'naughty' as these will only make him feel more insecure.

* Reinforce his good behaviour with lots of encouragement and praise, with much emphasis on the times he plays nicely with the baby and other toddlers.

* Be extra vigilant when he is in group situations and quickly divert his attention when he shows signs of frustration and irritability.

* Never leave your toddler alone with a baby for even a few minutes, and when they are together keep them in full view.

Assertiveness rather than violence

Dr Richard C. Woolfson advises that, despite your disapproval of violence, you still want your child to stand up for himself in the nursery, in the school playground and at home with his brothers and sisters. Quite rightly, you want him to be assertive so that he isn't pushed around by anyone. But there is a big difference between an assertive child and a violent or aggressive child.

Assertiveness means being able to express a point of view firmly, without generating violence. It is your child's ability to speak up for himself, to express his views confidently and clearly, but without threatening the listener. An assertive child, for instance, says, 'No, I'm playing with this toy right now, but I'll give it to you when I've finished,' and if he can say this with a smile and a calm voice then so much the better. Assertiveness enables him to achieve his goal without creating hostility.

Assertiveness will help your child find a non-violent solution to conflict. It is a combination of self-belief, clear thinking, independent thought and a sensitive personality. These are personal qualities you probably wish to encourage in your growing child anyway, so teaching him to be assertive shouldn't be too difficult.

Top tips for developing assertiveness

* Empathy – ask your child to think how he would feel if someone was violent towards him. Try to focus his attention on the feelings of the victim.

* Explanation – tell your child about the negative effects of his violent behaviour. Explain, for instance, that others would play with him more if he wasn't so aggressive.

* Caring – talk about the importance of helping others. The more caring he is towards other children and adults, the less likely he is to be violent towards them.

* Suggestion – offer ways that he could react to others without aggression. For instance, he could use a lighter tone in his voice, or he could say it with a natural smile.

* Speech – teach him to speak in a less confrontational way. For instance, 'If you tidy the crayons, I could put my game there' is better than 'Clear up that terrible mess!'

Other non-violent strategies

Help your child develop a range of conflict-resolution skills. For a start, encourage him to verbalise his feelings and to emphasise resolution. He could feel, for instance, 'I wish we weren't angry with each other, so we should try to get this sorted.' Your child will find his own words to express this feeling, especially if you practise this with him at home.

Show how to listen to the other person. Genuine listening means giving the other person a chance to speak, whereas children typically like to speak over anyone they don't want to hear. Explain that your child should give the other person time to say what they want. Listening also involves making eye contact and giving feedback (for instance, nodding at an appropriate moment). Again, these are skills you can practise with him at home.

Encourage your child to think of possible solutions to

the conflict. For instance, if he and his friend fight over a toy, they could agree for one of them to play with it for a couple of minutes and then the other can have a turn playing with it. Or if they argue over which DVD to watch, they could watch one DVD and then watch the other. It doesn't take much to find a suitable solution; all it needs is a bit of creative thinking.

Case study: Isabella, aged 18 months
Problem: Hitting her sisters, parents and other children
Cause: Attention-seeking

Isabella was very much a contented little baby for the first year of her life. She was a good eater and sleeper, with a sunny nature and ready smile. She had two older sisters of four and six and was the much-loved baby of the family. For her first year and a half she was the easiest and most loving child, adored by her big sisters and her parents.

At about 18 months Isabella began to hit her sisters. She was a very happy little girl but tended to resort to smacking her sisters if she wanted their attention. Both elder girls were naturally gentle and never once retaliated. Soon after this, Isabella began to hit her parents. Isabella's mother would pick Isabella up for a cuddle or kiss, and Isabella would use both hands to smack her mother's cheeks, as if she was clapping. Her mother had never had to deal with this sort of problem before. She was baffled, since her older daughters had never demonstrated this behaviour, and when she had seen other children being physically *unpleasant she had always thought the parents were responsible for not being firmer.*

Isabella's mother had never smacked Isabella or her sisters, although when her elder daughters were toddlers she did sit them on a 'naughty stair' on the rare occasions when they were repeatedly naughty. She was soon to discover that the 'naughty stair' had no effect on Isabella, and her toddler found this 'punishment' such fun that she would often hit her sisters and then run to the naughty stair as if it was a game.

Isabella's mother sought my advice when Isabella began to hit other children. She recognised that the first couple of times when Isabella had smacked her sisters the family had been mildly amused by their baby's feisty character. She also recognised that since Isabella was the youngest and much-adored baby of the family they had all been rather more indulgent to and tolerant of her exuberant behaviour than was sensible. While Isabella's mother recognised that this behaviour was not uncommon in toddlers, she was concerned that the more she tried to prevent Isabella hitting, the more amused her child seemed to be. Her mother also felt it was very unfair on her elder daughters that they had to put up with this when they were so kind and patient to their little sister. We discussed the fact that Isabella adored being the centre of attention and that as a bright child she had discovered that hitting was an immediate way to have everyone's attention. I commended Isabella's mother for not resorting to smacking, since we both felt that it is inappropriate to smack a child when the lesson you are trying to teach is that it was wrong to hit.

The first advice I gave to Isabella's mother was that the next time Isabella hit her or her sisters, all the family should firmly say, 'No, Isabella', and then avoid eye contact. It was important to be very clear that this was not a game and that her naughty behaviour would not be rewarded with attention. Secondly, I encouraged Isabella's mother to defuse situations where Isabella was able to hit her sisters. If her sister was lying on the floor when Isabella hit her, I suggested she immediately tell her elder daughter to put herself out of reach – sitting up in a chair or going to her bedroom. Similarly, if Isabella hit her mother during a cuddle, her mother was to put her down and immediately turn her attention to something else.

Within a week, the family's new response to Isabella's hitting was having a good effect. Isabella still occasionally hit her family, but having discovered it didn't produce a very interesting response, her hitting had become less common and more half-hearted.

Finally, I encourage her mother to tell Isabella that she would have to go to her cot if she repeated her behaviour. Isabella's mother was concerned this would affect Isabella's happiness in her cot, since she had always been very good about going to bed, and loved lying and playing in her bed. However, I reassured her that it was very unlikely that she would need to put Isabella in her cot more than once or twice, so there was little chance that this would affect her good sleep associations with it.

On the next occasion when Isabella hit her sister Isabella's mother gathered her up and carried her to her cot, where she was left for a couple of minutes.

Isabella was astonished and upset. She understood that this was the result of her hitting her sister. She began to cry and shout 'orry' – her word for 'sorry'. Her mother gave her a big cuddle and asked her to give her big sister a kiss.

Isabella is now nearly two and has not hit anyone in her family or social circle for more than two months. She is a delightful, loving little girl whose behaviour is no longer marred by episodes or hitting her sisters, parents or friends.

Dealing with tantrums in public

If your child has a tantrum when you're out and about, whether it's in the middle of the street, in the supermarket or in a restaurant, it can leave you feeling very embarrassed. Other people may seem to be judging you when your child is screaming, red-faced and angry in a public place, and it can be hard to respond in the way that you normally would when you have an unsympathetic audience. You may feel as if others are making disparaging judgements about your parenting skills, and people do sometimes make comments about children behaving badly in public, particularly if an incident occurs in a quiet environment.

Sometimes tantrums in public places can be avoided with some forethought – an afternoon trailing round the shops is not much fun for a small child, and once he starts to get tired or hungry you are more likely to encounter problems. I often see parents giving in to their child almost immediately when tantrums occur in public places, and in the short term it may feel easier to let your child get his own way. Children pick up on this very quickly, and if they know they can get what they want by causing a scene in public, they will do this.

The following guidelines may help:

* Children do need to let off steam and get some fresh air every day. If your child is cooped up inside every day and only gets out in the buggy or in the car, he is going to get frustrated. Letting toddlers have a run around in a park or playground will give them the opportunity to be boisterous and noisy, and means they are likely to be contented with more peaceful activities at home.

* A tired child will often misbehave in public, and you can avoid this by making sure you don't interrupt his regular routine too much when you are out and about. If he is overtired, he will get cross and unhappy.

* Hunger is another common source of problems when you are out and about with your toddler. Be prepared and take some healthy snacks out with you, as this can often nip the problem in the bud.

* Don't be unrealistic and expect your toddler to spend hours on end sitting happily in his buggy while you are out, or to be peacefully occupied at a table in a restaurant during a lengthy lunch with friends. Take some toys, books, pencils and paper.

* Consider leaving your toddler with your partner or another relative or friend if you are going on a lengthy shopping trip.

* If your child misbehaves in public, don't ignore the behaviour or give in to him because you feel embarrassed. It is important to deal with things in just the way

that you would at home. Otherwise your child will soon learn that he can get away with bad behaviour when you are out and about.

* Try not to worry about what other people might think if your child has a tantrum in public. Most parents have experienced this at some time or another, and will understand how you are feeling!

Conclusion

I hope that the guidance and suggestions offered in this book will help you both manage and avoid problems with your toddler. Understanding why tantrums happen will help you deal with them effectively and minimise any stress and worry they may cause.

The toddler years present a steep learning curve for both parent and child, and a deeper insight into the challenges and delights of this special period will enrich your experience. But it is not rocket science. It is my belief that the simple combination of a safe and happy home, a healthy diet, a good routine, encouragement and love will successfully result in your baby becoming a confident child.

Useful Resources

Allergy UK
Helpline: 01322 619 898
www.allergyuk.org

Blackout blinds, complete blackout kits, roller blinds,
temporary blinds, blackout material
Available from www.easyblindsonline.co.uk

The Foundation for the Study of Infant Deaths (FSID)
Helpline: 0808 802 6868
www.fsid.org.uk

The Great Little Trading Company
Tel: 0844 848 6000
www.gltc.co.uk

So Baby Limited
Tel: 01829 772 555
www.so-baby.co.uk

Soil Association
Tel: 0117 314 5000
www.soilassociation.org

Sure Start
Tel: 08002 346 346
www.direct.gov.uk/surestart

Twins and Multiple Births Association (TAMBA)
Tel: 01483 304 442
Twinline: 0800 138 0509
www.tamba.org.uk

UNICEF
Tel: 0844 801 2414
www.unicef.org.uk

Visit Gina Ford's website: www.contentedbaby.com

Further Reading

Ferber, Richard *Solve Your Child's Sleep Problems* (Dorling Kindersley, 1986)

Ford, Gina *The Complete Sleep Guide for Contented Babies and Toddlers* (Vermilion, 2006)

Ford, Gina *The Contented Toddler Years* (Vermilion, 2006)

Ford, Gina *The New Contented Little Baby Book* (Vermilion, 2006)

Green, Christopher *Toddler Taming* (Vermilion, 2001)

Morse, Elizabeth *My Child Won't Eat* (Penguin Books, 1988)

Nelsen, Jane *Positive Discipline: The First Three Years* (Prima Publishing, 1998)

Pearce, Professor John *The New Baby and Toddler Sleep Programme* (Vermilion, 1999)

Weissbluth, Marc *Healthy Sleep Habits, Happy Child* (Vermilion, 2005)

Woolfson, Richard C. *What is My Baby Thinking* (Hamlyn, 2006)

Contented Baby Newsletter

To learn more about the Contented Baby routines and Gina Ford's books visit Gina's official websites at www.contentedbaby.com and www.contentedtoddler.com and sign up to receive Gina's free monthly newsletter, which is full of useful information, tips and advice as well as answers to questions about parenting issues and even a recipe or two.

You may also want to take the opportunity to become part of Gina's online community by joining one or both of the websites. As a member you'll receive a monthly online magazine with a personal message from Gina, along with a selection of the latest exclusive features on topical issues from our guest contributors and members.

You'll be able to access more than 2,000 frequently asked questions about feeding, sleeping and development answered by Gina and her team, as well as many case histories not featured in the Contented Little Baby series of books.

www.contentedbaby.com

www.contentedtoddler.com

www.contentedbaby.com/shop-directory.htm

Contented Baby Consultation Service

Gina offers a one-to-one personal telephone consultation service for parents who wish for specialist help in establishing healthy feeding and sleeping habits, as laid out in the Contented Baby and Toddler routine books. If you would like further details of how a personal consultation with Gina works, we would request that in the first instance you send a detailed feeding and sleeping diary for 48 hours, along with a concise summary of what you think your problem is, using the contact form on www.contentedbaby.com.

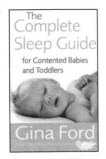